# *A Wilder In The West*

## The Story of
## Eliza Jane Wilder

edited by William Anderson

## Foreword

Bringing together the threads of a life lived in its prime a century ago is similar to following the path of a friend who moves away to other scenes: there are fallow periods in communication, sudden flurries of information, biographical gaps and coincidental, unexpected meetings. But somehow in the final analysis, available knowledge crystallizes into an overall estimation. Such has been the process of tracing the life of Eliza Jane Wilder.

She is known to the legions of "Little House" book readers (and was eventually written into scripts of **Little House on the Prairie** television episodes which dutifully used actual names but not real events or characterizations). But Eliza Jane lived a life which became a topic of public interest years after her death. Were it not for her brother Almanzo's writer-wife Laura Ingalls Wilder, Eliza Jane's name would have joined the ranks of the "hidden women"--who capably made homes, reared children and contributed to their localities in the latter part of the last century. Since her status as a supporting character in the "Little House" classics came long after she was gone, the records of her life had simply become family keepsakes--not historical documents--and memories garnered by her family from Eliza Jane herself were sketchy and hardly anticipated as future facts surrounding a literary character.

Central to this publication is the manuscript recounting Eliza Jane's Dakota homesteading. It is the nucleus of this study: engrossing sidelights to the pioneer experience and a paeon to the female influence in the rough-and-tumble of western settlement. I am indebted to Eliza Jane's grandchildren for their willingness to share their grandmother's account, the original of which is now among the relics of the Laura Ingalls Wilder Memorial Society in DeSmet, South Dakota.

Helping to piece together the homesteading story and the before-and-after of Eliza Jane's vigorous life have been her granddaughter Bettie Thayer Huey and the wife of her grandson, Elaine D. Thayer. Other Wilder relatives have been of great assistance . . . in Malone, New York, Dorothy B. Smith helped re-create the North Country origins of the family and from California has come much information on their "Aunt E.J." from Gladys Wilder, her brother James Wilder and his wife Thelma.

On the Dakota prairie in DeSmet, where Eliza Jane sought to set up home, contributions have come from many sources ... from Alma Abrahamson, enthusiastic researcher; from Vivian Glover and Vera McCaskell for assorted sleuthing and homestead locating; from Laura and Aubrey Sherwood and from **The DeSmet News**. And from South Dakota State University comes Dr. Ruth Alexander's introductory remarks which apply her expertise in women's studies and the homesteading era to one of the many female participants of the grand adventure, Eliza Jane Wilder.

W.T.A.
March, 1985

# Introduction

Like many another young woman of some education and much courage, resolution, and energy, Eliza Jane Wilder homesteaded alone in Dakota Territory. Fortunately for the reader one hundred years later, she left a written record of her experience when she submitted her story to the Department of the Interior as an affidavit of her good faith settlement on her claim. The narrative is far more than a recital of the bare facts of her adventure, for Eliza Jane recorded her feelings, hardships, hopes, disappointments and accomplishments.

The phenomena of the single woman homesteader has been documented by researchers of women in the west who have examined many of the narratives. Studies such as Sheryl Patterson-Black's "Women on the Great Plains Frontier"[1] and Glenda Riley's "Farm Women's Role in Agricultural Developments in South Dakota"[2] analyze some of the published and unpublished accounts of single women homesteaders. Estimates of the number of these enterprising females vary but all validate the fact that they existed in substantial numbers. One scholar claims that one third of the homesteads in the Dakotas were held by women in 1887;[3] another maintains that they represent between five and fifteen percent of the homesteaders between 1887 and 1908.[4] Some two hundred and twenty single women (including widows and married women living alone) filed claims in South Dakota between 1900 and 1915,* and more than sixty percent of them proved up their claim.[5]

The publication of Eliza Jane Wilder's account adds to the growing body of literature written by some of these women. Most the stories are unpublished manuscripts, such as Eliza Jane's, that have recently been made available to the popular reader. Such writers did not think they were writing for posterity but they felt their lives as homesteader were significant enough to be recorded on paper. Examples of such work with which Eliza Jane's might be compared are the published memoirs of Grace Fairchild in **Frontier Women.**[6] This persistent woman homesteaded with her husband West of the Missouri River in 1902 but ranches alone successfully to support herself and her family after her marriage failed. Another example is the publication of Bess

---

*Among the female homesteaders during this last rush was Carrie Ingalls of DeSmet, who dutifully spent six months yearly on a desolate claim north of Philip near a "town" named Elbon, which was duly named for a Mr. Noble, spelled in reverse.*

Corey's letters to her family about her homesteading experience west of Pierre, South Dakota, in 1909.[7] The best known published narrative is the book **Land of the Burnt Thigh** by Edith Eudora Kohl which recounts the homesteading adventure of the Ammons sisters west of Pierre in 1907.[8]

Like Eliza Jane, all of them took other jobs to insure survival while proving up their claims. The most frequent means of employment was teaching in a rural school, which is what Eliza Jane, "Bachelor Bess" Corey, and Grace Fairchild did. Grace Fairchild also took in boarders and "Bachelor Bess" cooked, sewed, and cleaned as well as taught to keep body and soul together. The Ammons sisters printed a frontier newspaper and ran a post office and general store.

Also like Eliza Jane, these women enjoyed their experience as pioneers, in spite of privations, hardships, and physical discomforts. They relished the indepedence of owning their own homes, however humble, and the challenge of farming and ranching under difficult circumstances. "Life was hard, but there was always something happening. I loved living on a homestead after I got settled down . . ." wrote Grace Fairchild.[9] The Ammons sisters described their social life with neighbors, especially other women, from miles across the prairie. On their very first day on the claim three "girl homesteaders" in shirtwaists and divided skirts called on them, riding stride a total of eighteen miles simply to "drop-in."[10] Bachelor Bess said she never had a better meal than the sardines and crackers she ate the first night after moving into her claim shack. No doubt, they all would have agreed wholeheartedly with Eliza Jane when she said, "I count the hardships as nothing compared with the happiness of having made for myself a home."

Hardships there certainly were! Snow on her head, backbreaking work, crop failures, ignorance of building skills and insect control, and illness plagued her venture. Loneliness, the enemy of so many women on the prairie, also troubled her--"the utter silence and loneliness of the situation grew so terrible as to be almost unendurable and I think I fathomed the depth of the word **Alone,**" she writes. She endured the October blizzard of 1880, but escaped before the storm blocked the railroad cuts making residents of the DeSmet prairie almost desperate for food and fuel.

In spite of all the difficulties, Eliza Jane clung to her home that she had so doggedly established on the prairie. She planted and weeded, cared for her ailing sister and her children, sold books, weathered the harsh Dakota climate, in order to keep her homestead going. After five years, she was near exhaustion, ". . . .but I had become very much attached to my little house . . . and I could not give it up." Yet ultimately, she did have to sell out.

This generous-spirited plucky heroine is not at all the image of the teacher "Miss Wilder" that her famous sister-in-law Laura Ingalls Wilder describes in **Little Town on the Prairie.** In the eyes of her pupil, young Laura, Miss Wilder appeared haughty and unfair, unable to maintain order in her schoolroom. She is taunted by her students who discover the childhood name that had so humiliated her and that she hated -- "lazy, lousy, Liza Jane."

In her own story, Eliza Jane discusses her teaching not at all. In fact, she indicates that she took the school in town very unwillingly and found the autumn term exhausting as she struggled to get the harvesting done and be hospitable to her sister and nephew who had come to visit. The reader might reconcile the differences in these two pictures by remembering that Eliza Jane's account was written from her point of view much closer to the actual events. Laura Ingalls Wilder's were nostalgic reminiscences of her childhood on the prairie and she viewed the world through the vision of the young Laura.

Eliza Jane has provided a lively account of her experience as a single woman venturing out to the Dakota frontier to make her own way. Her works makes abundantly clear that women were pioneers, too, and participated in the great enterprise of settling of the west in ways that have been largely ignored by western historians.

*Dr. Ruth A. Alexander*
*Chairman, English Department*
*South Dakota State University*
*Brookings, South Dakota*

## Footnotes

[1]*Sheryl Patterson-Black, "Women Homesteaders on the Great Plains Frontier,"* **Frontiers,** *I, 2, Spring 1976, pp. 67-88.*

[2]*Glenda Riley, "Farm Women's Roles in the Agricultural Development of South Dakota," South Dakota History, XIII, 1 and 2, Spring-Summer, 1983, pp. 83-121.*

[3]*Mary W.M. Hargreaves, "Women in the Agricultural Settlement of the Northern Plains,"* **Agricultural History,** *50, Jan., 1976, p. 182.*

[4]*Patterson-Black, p. 6.*

[5]*Paul Nelson,* **No Place for Clinging Vines: Women Homesteaders on the South Dakota Frontier,** *Unpublished Master's Thesis, University of South Dakota, 1978, p. 4.*

[6]*Grace Fairchild,* **Frontier Woman The Life of a Woman Homesteader on the Dakota Frontier,** *edited by Walker Wyman (River Falls, Wisconsin: University of Wisconsin Press), 1972.*

[7]*Paul Corey, "Bachelor Bess: My Sister,"* **South Dakota Historical Collections,** *Volume 37, pp. 4-101.*

[8]*Edith Eudora Kohl,* **Land of the Burnt Thigh** *(New York: Funk and Wagnalls, 1938).*

[9]*Fairchild, p. 73.*

[10]*Kohl, p. 5.*

[11]*Corey, p. 22.*

**Eliza Jane ... "a fashionable figure"**

## J. North County Beginnings, with Western Leanings!

*Eliza's voice was vehement in the kitchen. A fashionable figure in the French calico she had worn to town that afternoon, bangs frizzed above her narrow forehead and earrings swinging, she smacked plates onto the blue tablecloth.*

*"I was never so mortified in all my born days!" she asserted.*

*"Eliza, go look it up in the dictionary," their mother said placidly... "N,a,nay; B,o,b,bob. Nanbob... It means an East Indian potentate, rich beyond the dreams of avarice and living in the lap of luxury."*

*"I stepped into the bank this afternoon to deposit the egg money, and Mr. Holcomb came out of his office taking extra pains to be affable. 'And how be you all these fine days, Mrs. Wilder?' says he and says I, "Why Mr. Holcomb, says I, 'we're living like nabobs.' Eliza was with me, and no sooner on the sidewalk than, says she, the word's outlandish. I mortified her, says she. Be that it may, according to Noah Webster we're living like nabobs." -- from* **Free Land**, *by Rose Wilder Lane*

Rose Wilder Lane's weaving of a remembered family anecdote--the Nabob story--into her 1938 best-seller **Free Land** capsulized two important aspects of her father's family: that their careful nurture of the Malone, New York farm yielded a bountiful, bucolic life-style and that the centerpiece of the family unit was often the busy-bee bossy, spirited, sometimes-exasperating daughter named Eliza Jane, known by her own insistence as E.J.

1

Rose Lane knew E.J. as an indomitable aunt, a figure she admired, perhaps emulated and ultimately used more than once as a character in her fiction-writing. Her mother, Laura Ingalls Wilder--herself a strong personality--found E.J. insufferable as a teacher and someone to hardly endure as a sister-in-law later on. "I never did like Eliza Jane much" Laura had to admit when her "Little House" readers, aware of the animosity of the teacher-pupil relationship in **Little Town on the Prairie**, wrote her to wonder how they fared when related by marriage. Since both Rose's and Laura's characterizations of their relative are on record in their books, it seems that Eliza Jane's own story should be told in her own words. Her homesteading account, sandwiched between these biographical settings, will add Eliza Jane's own viewpoint to the persona created by her niece and her sister-in-law.

***

Eliza Jane was the third child of James and Angeline Wilder; a sister Laura (born 1844) and brother Royal (born in 1847) were already wandering the fields and barns and rooms of the red farmhouse on the farm five miles from Malone, New York when their sister was born in 1850. Oddly, of the six Wilder children, no exact birth date of Eliza Jane remains.* Three more children joined the family circle after Eliza Jane was born: a sister, Alice born in 1853; a brother Almanzo, born in 1857; and in 1869 when the other Wilders were young adults, the last son Perley, was born.

Life was an ordered, seasonal round of farming demands for the Wilder family on their northern-Adirondack acres; thrift, hard work, determination and high expectations were what Angeline and James exemplified for their children. They regarded their family farm as a pleasant melding of life-styles: they had country life, an appreciation for church and school and social life in the town of Malone.** But most of all, they saw the farm as a well-paying business. They lived well from the fruits of the farm, but the farm also paid cash money, banked to earn interest as soon as it was collected. And the Wilder

*The Wilder Family Bible, remembered by Gladys Wilder as a large, weighty volume, was destroyed, along with much other family memorabilia brought from Minnesota to Louisiana by James and Angeline, when the Perley Wilder home burned in 1930.

**For more detailed accounts of the Wilders and their lives in New York, Minnesota, Missouri, South Dakota and Louisiana, refer to Dorothy Smith's **The Wilder Family Story** and to this editor's **The Story of the Wilders,** both available from the Laura Ingalls Wilder Memorial Society, DeSmet, S.D.

children saw their mother as their father's equal partner in the business of the farm. The examples of the Wilder style of farm life influenced Eliza Jane and helped to nurture her strong character and independent nature.

Though devoted to agriculture, the Wilder parents were both descended from families who prided themselves on educating their offspring in the best fashion that circumstances would allow. Thus, when Laura, Royal, Eliza Jane, Alice and Almanzo were old enough to be sent down the road to the country school-house they went. Then their parents sent them. Their parents sent them to the Franklin Academy in Malone as boarding students. The Academy was one of the first schools of higher education in the North Country of New York State and the three-storied stone building was a proud structure.

While attending the Academy, E.J.--as she urged all to address her--decided to become a teacher. She taught her first school at nineteen and would rely on the profession for another dozen years and retained something of her classroom martinet demeanor for a life-time. Teaching alternated with stints back home on the farm, during which times E.J. slipped easily into the role of dairy-maid, cook, housekeeper, gardener, tender of hens and seamstress--all the domestic occupations she had been reared to and accepted as part of her life. She enjoyed giving orders at home as well as in school; she could discourse on politics and did, and she felt the stirrings of strong opinions relating to women's rights and the female suffrage plank!

**The Wilder farmhouse in 1984. It is easy to picture this house covered with the original painted red siding and the front porch jutting out between the windows in the front. The kitchen wing extends in the back.**

*Almanzo's father had a friend who moved from New York to Western Minnesota. He liked it there and Mr. Wilder went out to visit him and look the place over.*

*Mr. Wilder liked it so well that he bought a farm near Spring Valley. The Wilder family moved to the new farm, all the family except Royal and Almanzo who stayed behind and ran the old place for a year.*

*At the end of the year, their father and mother were so well pleased with the new home that they sold the New York farm and Royal and Almanzo drove a team with a covered wagon there to Spring Valley. In those days, once people started going west they usually kept on, going, making stops along the way.*
*Laura Ingalls Wilder*

Laura's simple explanations of the Wilder family's move west covers the general events that occurred to transplant the family to Spring Valley, Minnesota in the early 1870s. It was a piecemeal process -- the transplanting of the six Wilder children, their parents, possessions and lives from the North Country they had always known to the fertile farmlands of eastern Minnesota. While James and Angeline were getting settled and establishing a new home in the west, they left the Malone farm in the capable care of their older children. And so, Eliza Jane, between teaching, was in charge of the household and the kitchen, where she cooked for her brother Royal who ran the farm for their father while he was in Spring Valley. Evidently at some point Almanzo also returned to assist, for his wife mentioned it. Though James and Angeline, and Alice, Almanzo, Perley and Laura were with their parents in Minnesota during the time Eliza and Royal managed the Malone farm, the family separation was only temporary. The Malone farm was finally sold in the spring of 1875 and the family all re-gathered there before finally completing preparations to return to Spring Valley and the west.

With the Wilders re-settled again in Minnesota, on a 90 acre plot quite close to the thriving town of 1200 called Spring Valley, life resumed its usual pattern of farmland seasons. The Wilders were welcomed to the community and seem to have been particularly active in the Methodist church, where Eliza Jane and her sister Alice were both baptized in 1874. Sister Laura had married that year, and presumably Eliza Jane picked up her teaching career, though no records exist to say where.

It is clear that the move of the Wilders to the west did spark the interest of the older children in homesteading even further on, bearing out Laura Ingalls Wilder's remark that "once people started going west, they usually kept on . . ." When Alice Wilder married Albert

4

Baldwin in 1879, they farmed in western Minnesota near Marshall. That same year, Almanzo's mother bought the farm adjoining the Baldwin's as an investment. Almanzo had wanted the land and planned to buy it "on time" from Mrs. Wilder, so he broke four acres, raised wheat, built a barn, dug a well and planted shade trees. The next year, Almanzo remembered, "when we could get homestead land [in Dakota] . . . I let mother have the Marshall land back and throde in the improve[ments] . . . she sold it . . . for fifteen hundred."

The 1879 land boom in the Dakota Territory, directly related to the building of the Chicago and Northwestern railroad line west, brought to fruition the plan of Eliza Jane and her brothers Royal and Almanzo to file on the "free land." Almanzo heard from a friend in St. Paul that the railroad division would end at a townsite called DeSmet, where the tracks were being laid on the empty prairie near the Silver Lake camp. Assuming that DeSmet would be a sizable town someday and a good location for a farm (the division ultimately ended in Huron, not DeSmet), Almanzo, Royal and a doctor friend left from Marshall to file on claims at Yankton, Dakota Territory in late summer of 1879. They were joined by Eliza Jane who was teaching in Valley Springs, a new settlement in the territory.*

With difficulties--especially ten miles west of Sioux Falls, where one of Almanzo's horses died of colic--the group reached Yankton and the land office. Knowing location of the town-site of DeSmet, the Wilders all took claims closest to it--Eliza Jane's adjoining the future town, Royal's the next claim north of his sister's, the doctor's west of Eliza's and Almanzo's further north. By paying the $14.50 filing fees, Royal, Almanzo and Eliza Jane had become Wilders of the West.

*Eliza Jane, well-educated woman, was an asset to the tiny frontier settlement and was well-liked in Valley Springs. Though she settled in DeSmet, she was a welcome visitor in her former hometown. Her autograph book "From her Sabbath School Class--Valley Springs, D.T., Merry Christmas 1881"is filled with good wishes of friends.

## JJ. *"A Brief Account . . . of myself, my endeavor, hopes and failures"*

*Editor's note: Just as in the possessions of many American families, there remained among the descendants of Eliza Jane Wilder a potpourri of old letters, documents, musty books and keepsakes representing a long life. The school books she used, the autograph book she passed around to friends, pictures of family and acquaintances and a clutter of memoriabilia gathered dust in the Thayer attics after E.J.'s death in 1930. Then, she was mother and grandma; soon she was to be a literary character in the "Little House" books.*

*Inspired by the fact that she had married one of Eliza Jane's grandsons and spurred on by interest in the family's connections with* **Farmer Boy** *Elaine Thayer of Louisiana (Mrs. Walter Thayer) started investigating the family tree in the 1960s. She had as her convenient source her father-in-law, Wilder Thayer, the only child of Eliza Jane and Tom Thayer. Elaine also began to contact other remaining Wilder relations: children, grandchildren and great-grandchildren of Perley, Alice, Laura and Royal Wilder. Gradually, the years following* **Farmer Boy** *were pieced together as Elaine Thayer continued to contact family members and researchers of the Wilder lore.*

*Elaine was naturally fascinated by Eliza Jane, her children's great-grandmother. That independent, sometimes domineering, bossy-but-admirable educator-homesteader-career woman loomed large among the lists of long-dead relatives. Her heritage, the story of this dauntless, spirited Wilder woman, seemed to cry for an interpreter when Wilder Thayer passed on to Elaine "all the material he could find on his parents, even his mother's manuscript of her experiences in the Dakotas."*

*Penned delicately in feathery, flowing browned ink on lined legal foolscap, Eliza Jane Wilder recounted her memorable stint as a Dakota homesteader from 1879 through 1885. The manuscript was headed with the weighty words: TO THE DEPARTMENT OF THE INTERIOR, WASHINGTON, D.C. It is prefaced with this explanation:*

> *"Being required by the Land Commission to make a full affidavit as to good faith in the matter of Homestead entry N. 30 ¼ Sec.[tion] 28 T.[ownship] 111 R.[ange] 56, I herein give a brief account of myself, my endeavor, hopes and failures since the spring of 1879."*

*The pages that followed re-tell in retrospect an intensely personal struggle as a woman alone, battling the fierce elements of the unbroken Dakota plains in the fight to win title of the available acres of government "free land." It is, observed DeSmet historian Aubrey Sherwood, "a tale of Job." While many a hearty masculine homesteader could not bear the burden of the hostile untamed land, the struggle was even more acute for the small but mighty band of females who went west to file homestead claims. Eliza Jane's narrative is such a testimony to the pluck and grit typical of the petticoat pioneers.*

*Eliza Jane's tale is not to be confused with a diary, though it is realted in a chronological fashion. It is a final, polished copy, cleanly drafted, and it is the opinion of this writer that she wrote her reminiscenses within a few years following the time she quit the western life in 1885. Perhaps she composed it in the lamplight of her boarding house quarters in Washington where she worked as a government clerk in 1890. Clearly, she did not fill the pages for mere pleasure, but with some purpose. Was she writing to the Department of the Interior to assist in swaying some policy of legislation pertaining to the Homestead Act? Scattered scraps of evidence do reveal that Eliza Jane remained vitally interested in the plight of the prairie homesteader, even after abandoning the life herself. Or was she called upon to testify to some committee interested in eyewitness accounts of conditions in the Dakotas? History does not say, but the tone and style of her writing indicate that Eliza Jane was writing to convince and draw an accurate picture of the rigors of acquiring "free land."*

*Happily, Eliza Jane kept the Dakota manuscript all her life, through many travels and many circumstances. When it passed to her grandson's wife, its future was assured. Carefully, Elaine Thayer transcribed what she could of the confusing handwriting. With each anecdote illustrating her challenges in homesteading life, Eliza Jane established herself as an resourceful, competent and likeable spokesperson for the "gentlewoman farmer" of her era. Elaine not only hoped to see the story preserved for her own family, but for the family of "Little House" readers who would enjoy hearing the words of the sister-school-teacher of* **Farmer Boy** *and* **Little Town on the Prairie**.

*In 1971, the "E.J." manuscript was sent to this writer, who perceived its appeal to "Little House" fans and as another point of view in the experience of Laura Ingalls Wilder called "the fascination and the terror" of homesteading. While Laura viewed the carving out of frontier farms in Kingsbury County, Dakota from the viewpoint of a*

7

*pioneer's daughter, Eliza Jane saw it all as a fledgling farmer, a woman with the goal of creating a home and often overwhelmed by the forces of nature. And readers of* **Little Town on the Prairie** *are painfully aware of Laura's hostility and antagonism toward her teacher Miss Wilder — who would ironically become her sister-in-law.*

*Eliza Jane Wilder's voice deserved to be heard.*

*In 1972, the first edition of* **A Wilder in the West** *appeared, the premiere publication in Wilder lore of the quickly expanding Laura Ingalls Wilder Memorial Society of DeSmet. The little book has, over the years, brought that needed new viewpoint to Eliza Jane's character, as well as added to the records the strivings of a pioneer woman who perservered against a fierce, resistant land.*

*Here, a century later, with new background and supporting research, Eliza Jane tells her story . . .*

## *J Had The Great Desire To Secure A Home*

In April, 1879, I went to Dakota Territory to begin an engagement to teach one year in the school at Valley Springs. I had the great desire and ambition since childhood to secure a home of my own. I began teaching when 19 and all that I could save of my salary each year I had banked at interest.

In August 1879, I left Valley Springs in a carriage for Yankton to file upon a homestead. The first night out we found very comfortable quarters at a farmhouse the owner of which very kindly made for themselves a bed on the kitchen floor that I might enjoy such comfort as their sleeping rooms afforded.

The second day the driver was urging his horses to do their best that we might reach Yankton before stopping for the night when I noticed one horse sweating profusely. I called his attention to the matter but he replied twas only the heat of the day, which with the rapid driving caused the horse to sweat profusely. I was not satisfied. I spoke again and the same moment the horse became covered with foam. The driver gave the reins to a gentleman sitting beside him saying, "Do not let them stop." He jumped from the carriage and began unfastening the harness. As soon as he loosened the traces he led the horse away and she fell into a convulsive agony and in less than an hour her sufferings were ended. We were 20 miles from Yankton and the only visible house being a sod dugout where an invalid boy about 16 with his little brother perhaps 8 years was staying, their parents having gone to Yankton.

It was useless to think of proceeding, we camped for the night. I slept in the carriage which was secured to the ground as well as possible by ropes and stakes, as a precaution against storms. Before morning a severe wind storm came, accompanied by vivid lightning and thunder which must be heard to be appreciated. The living horse was constantly calling for its mate. I had never seen even a chick die up to this time and you may imagine I slept little if any. But nothing daunted when daylight came we began preparations for a forward movement. Improved claims were far apart but we tried to obtain some sort of conveyance. It was useless. In harvest time neither love nor money would induce a farmer to leave his grain exposed to the caprice of the storm clouds for a day. So we proceeded with one horse fastened to the pole of the carriage, to the Land Office. I filed the homestead entry N. 20 ¼, Sec. 28, T. 111, R 56, also a timber claim about two miles from Hd. And returned to Valley Springs where for a few weeks I was quite ill with the thought of that dying horse and all the hardships of the trip had an unusual effect upon the nervous system. But I recovered and was ready for the fall term of school.

* * *

*In 1937, when Rose Wilder Lane was researching material to use in her upcoming* **Saturday Evening Post** *serial and subsequent novel* **Free Land,** *she recalled the trek west of her father, her Aunt E.J. and Uncle Royal. Wishing to use the incident in her fiction, she wrote her parents from Columbia, Missouri where she was living at the Tiger Hotel, asking for particulars. Both Laura and Almanzo replied:*

*Wrote Laura:*

*As for getting Manly to tell what someone said—Have you heard of oysters? [Almanzo's quiet, unassuming ways were his dominant nature]. It is long ago. But you can imagine what E.J. would say to make him drive faster. You must see the picture of the long, hard drive. 150 miles is a long way with a team, the dry noon lunch, the eager drinking at the windmill and all the rest. Picture the prairie with no settlement, no least sign of "Human habitation" for mile after mile, the hope of a good investment to urge them on, or perhaps a home ... Imagine the loss of such a valuable horse to a poor man, making a start in the west and the courage and resourcefulness needed to go on and make a success in spite of "Hell and high water." There was not whining in those days, no yelling for help. A man did what he could with what he had.*

*And Almanzo added his point of view to the story of the trip west to Yankton with his brother and sister:*

*... In a ½ days drive south west as we went farm houses got quite thin ... lots of open spaces ... a horse with the colic will lay down and roal and git up & lye down just about as fast as it can until they*

*get some medison to stop the gas or die. A horse cannot pas wind off the stomac through the moth like a person does & if thear bowels are stopped thear troubles are soon over . . . First simptoms you notice its sides are swolen and in a minet or to it wants to stop & they will usualy try to role but never . . . clear over Just roll part way up then as they roll back so thear feet tuch the ground they get up amedietly lie down & it is up and down till the medison relieves them or till they are dead. [Spellings are preserved as in Almanzo's original letter of April 4, 1937.]*

\* \* \*

## J Went To My Claim . . . Expecting To Remain Forever

I hired a man\* to build me a house on my claim which he did in October or November of 1879. I do not know which. Taking with him his plow and such lumber as was indispensible. The "House" was 8 × 10 or 10 × 12. I am not sure. Built of four walls made by piling sod or turf obtained by plowing the soil. A post in the center supported a crossbeam which rested at either end upon the sod walls. The end walls higher than the side. The roof was made by putting pieces of 2 × 4 from this cross piece to the side walls and covering the whole with hay tied in bundles. The window was small, 4 panes of glass, a frame having been set in the sod wall to receive it, the door was opposite the window, the chimney was built of sod.

Knowing I must establish a residence within six months of date of filing, I brought the matter before the school board and they granted the usual December vacation in November. And I went, I think, 150 miles in a lumber wagon, there being no roads fit for lighter carriages. Slept in the wagon while enroute. Took with me a small stove that cost $5.00. Trunk with some clothing. We spent the vacation there and returned to the engagement at Valley Springs, leaving my stove, etc. to show the land seekers that the claim was already taken. And indeed I regarded it as my home and looked forward eagerly for the time when I should be at liberty to return. I seemed imperative that I should finish my engagement and obtain my salary as the money previously earned was loaned for a term of years and only the interest was payable yearly.

In April, 1880, I think about the 15th, I again went to my claim expecting to remain forever. Indeed I even said should I die I want my body buried there. I was an enthusiast, as indeed were all whom I met there at that time. I counted the hardships as nothing compared with the happiness of having made for myself a home. The grade for RR was being made. Hundreds of men from the east were coming every

\*The "man" was actually E.J.'s brother Almanzo, who built four shanties that month, with help from Royal.

day on foot or by private conveyance, as workmen on the RR in every way, all seeking land. When I reached my claim there had been a sort of hotel built a half-mile or more from me and the landlady with her cook were the only ladies in the place. About 4 days after my return there came a sudden change of temperature and during the night a severe snow.* I had taken with me no furniture because having no home large enough to hold any except my stove, a small table and chair to two. The ground being cold and damp I did not dare sleep as I did in the fall and as there seemed nothing better to do I took the door from the hinges, drove stakes in the ground to support it and put my bed on, hanging a rubber blanket at the door-way. Of course the snow found ready egress to my house and in the morning it was on a level six inches higher than my bed.

I had been awake all night keeping the snow from my face. I thought I could not or dare not thus expose myself and applied for board at the hotel until such time as I could obtain a more satisfactory establishment of my own.

I found however that the snow was at least six inches deep in every room at the Hotel** and the only place for me to sleep was a lounge in the dining room. And there was no promise of privacy there as the rush of land seekers was so great that the night before just as many men as could be on the floor wrapped in their blankets had occupied even that room. I prepared my own quarters. Shoveled out the snow, rescued the stove and lived largely out of doors.

Early in May began breaking—think I paid $3.00 or $3.50 per acre. I had taken with me some seed corn, potatoes, etc. as well as food. And I cut the potatoes, followed the man who was breaking dropping the seed in the furrows for the next furrow to cover. After using up the potatoes I planted corn until that seed was gone.

Then I stopped breaking until later in the season. And made me a garden planting sweet corn, peas, beans, lettuce, etc. for I found opening a new home on the prairie very expensive. I feared unless I could get some return that my means of improving the place would be gone before I had a home.

I tended my garden faithfully, watered it when dry, kept down the weeds and everything grew finely. In June the cars reached us, and very soon my father came with a car, brought two cows, furniture, carpet bed and bedding, etc. With his help I built me a house, a tiny affair of course for I would not accept money from him and indeed he

*See Chapter 27, "Living in Town" in **By the Shores of Silver Lake** for Laura Ingalls Wilder's version of the same blizzard.

**"The Beardsley House," an early hotel in DeSmet.

could not afford to do more for me than he did. I did much of the work of building with my own hands from laying the floor to putting on shingles and of course I pounded my thumbs for I had never before learned to drive a nail. But what amount of hardship can daunt the spirit of a native born American?

My garden was growing finely and one day I took some lettuce to town and sold it for a quarter. (Here let me say that my garden was near the sod shanty while my new house being near the east line, was half a mile from my garden.) Thus making two miles walk and the caring of the lettuce. When I showed my father the .25 as the first fruits of my enterprise I shall never forget the look of sadness as he said, "Human nature is a capricious thing. You were not satisfied to work six hours per day in the school room at $2.00 but you are as delighted as a child with a new toy at receiving .25 in return for a mile walk in the hot sun aside from the labor of producing the lettuce."

## J Fathomed The Depth Of The Word "Alone"

The time came for him to return to his home. I bade him good bye bravely but dared not accompany him to the depot. And after he was out of sight the utter silence and loneliness of the situation grew so terrible as to be almost unendurable and I think I fathomed the depth of the word ALONE. But the Bean bugs were destroying the potatoes. And the only way to save the crop was to pick them off.

I had all the nervous horror of any lady with regard to bugs but I was determined to succeed so I worked picking off pails full and burning them but I was not equal to the task. They increased faster than I could kill them and I found either I was working too hard or for some other reason my strength was failing. I had been drawing water from the well to water the cows and one day I became so dizzy while drawing up the bucket that I fell and only by a narrow chance escaped falling into the well. I then went to a neighbor who had no cows and told him if he would come and milk and water them and move their picket rope when needed I would give him all the milk except what I needed for my own use.

He could not come that night so I returned, milked the cows and had just reached the house when a terrible thunder storm burst over us with strong winds. I was rejoicing that I had safely reached the house when I heard a noise and looking closely I found one cow had broken her rope and was frantic with fright trampling through the corn and I feared she would soon be lost. To seize a dish of salt and run to her was the act of impulse rather than thought. I found she had confidence in me and began to eat the salt. The rope was broken close to her head too short to tie. I remembered I had a trunk strap in the house but while I was getting it the cow ran again. However I secured her and tied her to a board that was securely nailed to the house. Of course I was for some time exposed to the storm.

In the morning Mr. O'Connel came and took charge of the cows. I told him of my two weeks fight with the bean bugs and he did not wonder at my illness as he said the bugs were very poisonous and showed me how to use Paris Green for the Potatoes. The beans were ruined but the corn looked well and I had had five more acres broken and sowed to buckwheat. The poison had entered my system and I continued to grow worse until I was confined to my bed for a few days during which time I paid $1.25 a day for a women to come and stay with me and could keep her only a few days at that. Of course I got better and I was not discouraged. I kept two loaded revolvers at the head of my bed all the time but never had occasion to use them.

**The still-empty, lonely acres of Eliza Jane's homestead land.**

### The Winter . . . A Matter Of History

In September I think the 5th there came a frost so severe as to kill grass. The corn was not ripe and of course ruined. The lobes of buck wheat were loosened and a strong wind the next day just threshed it where it stood. Thus every bit of crop was ruined in a night.

Was I discouraged, not a bit. I had potatoes left and hundreds of prairie chickens came to eat the buckwheat but I had no means of catching them. I wrote such bright descriptions of frontier life home that my Mother and little brother (Perley Day Wilder) a boy of 12 or 13 came out to see me. They were not charmed but then it was not their home. Mother wanted me to return with her for the Winter. But

**Eliza's "little brother" Perley...**

**"reached the barn everyday..."**

I declined. She also urged me to take advantage of the June 15th Act. But that would not result in improving the land and building up for myself a home.

During her stay came the October Blizzard. Of course we were not prepared for it. A young gentlemen from Minneapolis who had been out with my brother shooting and had stopped for tea was detained through the storm, a very unwilling prisoner. And he thought he had a hard time of it though we gave him the best we had. It so chanced we were nearly out of fuel and flour. And the storm raged with unabated fury three days. My brother reached the barn every day and indeed it was a merciful providence that sent to much aid at that time for had I been alone I fear I should have perished. As it was we obtained hay which we twisted for fuel. The cows were fed and our loss was only a few hens and chickens. But near us a man who had a fine span of horses dared not go to them and after the storm he found them literally buried in snow which had blown in through the window I think slightly ajar. They were dead. Hundreds of sheep and many cows and other stock loose on the prairies or in herds stampeded and were lost.

After the storm ceased we went to town but there was no fuel to be had. Neither was there a lb. of flour. Plenty ordered but stopped by the blockade. Someone told me that at the hotel they always kept a large supply and as it was not possible for transients to reach them until the trains came bringing supplies it might be I could get some there. I went and by persuasion obtained ten pounds for $1.00. Of course there was no use of argument with my mother, she would not leave Dakota unless I went with her. So I put such things as I valued most in Mr. O'Connel's house engaged him to care for my livestock and closed up my establishment but only a few months as I fully expected to return in February if not sooner. And it was not at my own desires that I left then.

14

The winter that followed is a matter of History. Very few more trains entered the territory that winter. It was ten days before the R.R. were opened after the October Blizzard and storm followed storm. The officials of the R.R. and the citizens along the route united in their efforts to keep it open but 'twas useless. In December they gave up the battle and from that time until May no trains reached DeSmet where my land is located. One family near my claim lived on boiled turnips for months. Mrs. Judge Barnes whose claim joins mine told me for six weeks they had nothing but wheat cracked in a coffee mill and made into mush with water for food. Neither butter, milk, sugar, tea, coffee, potatoes, or pork could be obtained and for a long time previous the merchants would sell but 1 lb. of sugar per week to a family. Kerosene was gone, light was obtained by burning a rag in a saucer of melted tallow. Hay was the only fuel to be obtained for months. During this time I was safe in my father's home but I was not strong the M.D. said there were symptoms of poisoning in my system. I told him of my battle with the bean bug and he seemed to be of the opinion that it would be some time until I fully recovered.

In March my sister (Laura Wilder Howard) was left with two children the youngest a babe. Her own health was such that for weeks we had to watch over her constantly.

## 1881-1882

In April my Mother's health failed and they seemed to think it was the over ruling hand of God which had kept me there when I was so greatly needed. They were both gaining rapidly when the blockade opened and as my sister had no means of support aside from my father I took the little girl (Angelina Howard) about 5 years old with me and returned home sometime before the 10th of May, 1881 on the first or second train that entered the Territory. I had my land seeded to wheat, a few acres in grass seed, more land broken, five acres of oats sown on my timber claim. And this year I put flax on my new breaking. As fast as money was due I collected it and denied myself every possible comfort that I might use more in improving my land. Obtained copying in the County Clerk's Office to pay for work being done. When the flax was well started I found mustard in the crop. That I could not permit so I went through the field again and again pulling every spear I could find for I could hire no one who could be trusted to do the work.

In August just when it seemed I was most needed at my place a message came to me from Mr. Jackson at Valley Springs saying his wife was thrown from a buggy and so seriously injured the M.D. had little hope of her recovery, and wished me to come to her at once. At first I thought I could not go but there was a strong attachment bet-

15

ween us and when I left her I had promised if ever needed and sent for me I would come if living so I took, in a satchel what I thought I would need for myself and niece for a few weeks. I did not think I could be gone over three weeks. But she recovered slowly and could not think of my leaving her. Indeed every time I spoke of going it brought on a return of nervous headaches when for days at a time she lay in a darkened room allowing no one but myself to be with her. Therefore I remained as nurse and friend until February, 1882 when I went home.

I gathered my possessions once more. There had been nothing stolen but the vinegar cask had frozen and burst and there had been much loss in many ways. The man who should have cut the flax of course waited for a convenient season and let the frost treat it as it had the buckwheat the year before. Then he cut it, stacked and threshed the straw. The expense was just the same as for a good crop and the returns nothing. The wheat was fairly good and nearly replaced the loss on the flax. If I remember distinctly, the bill for harvesting, threshing and hauling it to market and plowing the land ready for the springs crop exceeded the receipts for the grains by $20 to $25 leaving nothing for the expense of seeding. But still I was not

The DeSmet school as it appears today, a prominent site on the Wilder tour of "Little Town on the Prairie." E.J. taught in this building but on its original site two blocks east and north. By 1885 the school was far too small; it was already being called the "old" school-house and was moved to Third Street and converted into a home. It remains a residence today, but is readily identified as a standard one-room prairie school. A plaque identifies the historical structure; inside, while re-decorating, owners found the original blackboards under layers of wallpaper!

discouraged: I thought the land is so new and I was away. Next year will be better. So I had the corn planted on five acres, 2½ acres of potatoes and the rest wheat. On my timber claim five acres of wheat and five acres of boxelder trees planted. Attended to my garden and I found after leaving home the summer before another crop of mustard had grown and ripened seeding the whole farm. But with courage and resolution worthy of an abler foe I weeded the mustard from wheat, oats and flax alike.

In August the President of the school board came to me and wanted I should take the school for a year in town. I told him I could not, my home work required all my strength, but he persisted and said they had had no school worthy of the name since the school started and were unable to obtain a teacher fitted for the work. The result was I took the school but would not engage for a year only for one term for I knew I was certainly failing slowly but surely and found my health would not permit the whole year's work. I began the school in September 1882 with the understanding that I could continue the year if I wished.*

During this term of school my sister and little boy came; other friends came for a few weeks' visit. I could obtain no help in the house and it was only most persistant effort during every leisure moment that I obtained men to harvest the corn and potatoes.

When the term of school ended I was worn out and unfitted for any labor. My sister and I looked the situation over carefully. The house was poorly built and cold, exposed to the bitter prairie winds. The baby was not two years old. Her health was not good. My own was very badly strained. A sister in Minnesota and other friends were urging us to come to them. I had no rest from incessant toil often beyond my strength for 18 or 20 months. And we decided it best to take a vacation.

## *"J put out 2500 cuttings."*

She went to my sister's in Minnesota. I visited many different friends. Was snowbound some weeks at one place. Improved every opportunity for earning anything. My friends added to their invitations the cost of tickets and indeed paid all my expenses. It was a winter of rest and recuperation. I left home sometime after Thanksgiving 1882 and returned early in spring 1883. I had a good many young apple, cherry and plum trees, strawberries, currants, etc.

*See **Little Town on the Prairie,** *"Miss Wilder Teaches School."*

This spring I put in 25 catan—grapes, 200 raspberry plants, 100 currants and added largely to the shade trees about the house. Each year even in November, 1879, I had set out more or less trees as time and means would permit. I hired 10 acres broken on the homestead that spring. Five acres to potatoes, five to corn. The seed planted the year before on the timber claim did not grow. I could get no one to put in trees for me until after it would be too late to make it successful. So I went to the tree claim and put out 2500 I think, cuttings, the required number on five acres. The old land was rented. I was to have ⅓ the crop but the tenant was not responsible for the mustard.

**Gnarled trees planted by Eliza Jane on her tree claim.**

**Eliza Jane's tree claim today.**

It seems useless to me to tell all I did. The foregoing you must see that I left undone nothing I could do either by my own hands or hired labor to improve my home. I sold one cow and calf for $60, built a better house. The one that is now standing, two rooms below and a chamber, double board sided and tar paper double between the sheeting. Painted it white, virginia creepers over the windows, a flower garden, roses, verbena, phlox, etc., before the door. An arbor at the left over which a magnificent wild grapevine grew. A hen house with yard, etc. The men who rented my land had taken several hundred acres on different claims near me and in harvest they wanted to board with us. My sister and I decided we could do the work and took these five men while cutting the grain. They threshed from the field so we had 16 men ten days while threshing. Toward the last, sister's little boy was taken ill and required every minute of her time. I sent for a neighbor girl about 16 years of age and offered her $1 per day if she would come and wash the dishes. But when she knew those threshers were there she would not come. And I did the best I could alone. I mention this to show you how almost impossible it was to obtain help at that time. Every one had all they could do on their own land.

The crop was good but prices low. I had collected all moneys due me—sold my grain, paid up all bills for the summer and about the first of November 1884 I balanced bank accts. and found $30 to my credit.

## J Left Nothing Undone

Again my sister and I held a council of war. 'Twas bitter cold, $30 would go but a short ways towards fuel even, soft coal being $8-$10 per ton. But the house was comparatively warm. Plenty of pork and potatoes.

Of course there was no farm work to do while the ground was frozen. I told my sister if she would stay by the stuff I would go to work. She agreed. We got someone to take care of the cow. I took an agency for a bookseller. Bought a 1000 mile ticket for $25.00 and started for life or death. I had but $5.00 to pay expenses. But the Lord was on my side. I worked with the energy of despair and returned in three weeks with $100. I made several trips during the winter and spring, but none to exceed three or four weeks. After spring opened my sister was left alone with the children while I was delivering books. During this time the cow died. She could not endure the loneliness and really being very ill sent for me. I returned to find her nervous system entirely unstrung. After a few weeks she went to my father's leaving the children with me. It seemed imperative that she should have rest.

I had ordered quite a quantity of fruit from a N.Y. Nursery which I had set. Much of that previously set had died. That winter my grapes were killed though covered quite deep. My last cow was dead. My money was all gone. But I had a cozy home, walls nicely papered and floors all carpeted except for the kitchen and that painted. Cookstove and heater, pictures on the walls, lace curtains at the windows. The vines had lived and also the wild grapes. The hens were doing well and I felt sure of success in time. I continued improvement on my tree claim putting in trees where others had died and when I could hire no one to hoe I shouldered my own hoe, walked two miles and put in a full days work for myself.

**Laura Howard and children, after they had returned to Spring Valley from their experiences on Eliza's Dajota claim. To help raise cash, Laura had worked as a seamstress in DeSmet. Sewing by her side in the same dressmaking shop was her future sister-in-law, Laura Ingalls.**

I found careless cultivating had plowed out trees. And had the same trouble that falls to all women who undertake to become farmers. One day I was caught in a storm about ¾ of a mile from home. The wind blew so hard as to crush the Catholic Church* and several buildings were moved from their foundations. The town hall among the rest. Hail and rain came in torrents and with such force that my arms were black and blue after. Gardens were destroyed, wheat and other grains seriously injured. Some fields were never cut. But I faced the storm for over one half mile. My sister's children were home alone and I feared they might be seriously frightened else I should have stayed down on the ground, until it was over. Of course I took a severe cold which all the usual remedies failed to relieve. The Dr. could do me no good, but I thought it would wear off and kept at work as far as strength would permit.

*The DeSmet **Leader** of July 12, 1884 mentions the "terrible storm" and the "considerable damage." The report mentions, as E.J. did, "the unfinished Catholic Church blown down . . . the band hall moved about six feet and badly wrecked. . . ."

In October my sister wrote me she was better but not well and it seemed best not to expose herself to the rigors of another Dakota winter. She wanted me to bring her children to her. I therefore, sold my turkeys, found a man who would take my hens and chickens, nearly 100 and keep them through the winter for half. He would not guarantee their lives but 'twas the best I could do with them. I had then held my claim for over five years and regarded it as my own for I certainly felt that if any mortal had "paid dear for the whistle" I had. My lawyer told me that it made no difference about the final proof. The law required five years residence and one could then prove any time within seven years of date of original entry. But after the five years no one could jump the claim or contest my right. I will here say that in all the times of absence I had never feared trouble from any source except the "Land Fiend." I had regarded the government as a Friend to the actual settlers and willing to aid them in any honest endeavor to obtain a home.

I had long before this doubted being able to live very long in that climate but I had become very much attached to my little house and a fine class of people had located around us and I could not give it up.

## With deep regret J left my home . . .

In October, 1885 I took the children to my sister. And with deep regret I left my home for I feared I should never return. At the time I reached my father's I could not speak a loud word and coughed constantly sometimes two or three o'clock in the morning before I could get a moments' sleep for coughing. But I improved, obtained the use of my voice. The cough nearly ceased. I spent some time visiting an uncle in Minnesota and as soon as a reasonable degree of health returned I knew I should get better. I wanted money for my springs work in Dakota and I renewed my engagement as book agent. My success was not equal to the winter before. And a friend of mine, an old lady in Iowa needing someone, I went to stay with her. But the seeds of disease were in my system yet and a little overdoing brought me down on a bed of illness from which I did not recover until late in the spring.

My sister had decided her health was much better in Minn. than in Dakota and she could not return. But I went back alone, some time in May as soon as the M.D. would permit. I put what money I had left some $30 to $40 into breaking, rented the land for ⅓ the crop, hired my garden made even to the weeding of my flowers. Busied myself indoors with painting, embroidery, etc.

My friends were very glad to see me home again and seldom a day passed that one or more did not take a meal with me. But my sister and the children were gone. I was alone a great deal. The Dakota winds which I had braved were proving too much for me. I did not regain my strength.

About the middle of June I advertised for final proof*, which was made the 1st of August. And still I had not abandoned the hope of making that my future home. I went away intending to return in a few months at longest, just as soon as health would permit. The final receipt issued was recorded and everyone in our part of the world regarded it as good as a deed. The land is assessed and taxes levied same as tho I held the deed.

I left my carpets on the floor, books in the bookcase, bed made up and bedding securely packed, even a part of my own wardrobe. Flour, sugar, and food of that nature that would not spoil during a few months absence. Pork in the cellar. All my dishes, stoves, cooking utensils, furniture, etc. even looking glass and pictures hanging on the walls.

But my health did not improve. I kept gradually failing. Neither friends nor Physicians thought best for me to return to Dakota. My only means of support was my land. The returns in the fall of 1885 were $6. I had to borrow but obtained what I needed by giving my note. I could not mortgage my home.

My friends urged me to sell. I could see no other means of support. I wrote Barnes and Thomas of DeSmet to sell it. Then countermanded the instructions and again consented to sell. But when an actual purchaser was found I could not let it go. I felt sure could I but regain my health I should yet succeed in living there, but I grew worse constantly.

*Homesteaders were compelled to place legal notices in local newspapers stating that they had fulfilled residence requirements outlined by the Homestead Act, before obtaining their "patents" to quarter sections of "free land." Eliza Jane joined thousands of other happy homesteaders in this final requirement in the hard-won process of "proving up" claims. Elaborating on the process, Laura Ingalls Wilder wrote: "At 'proving up' the homesteader went to the Land Office with two witnesses to prove that for five years he had made a continuous residence on this claim, never being away from his home (house) there for more than six months. That he had a house on it and ten acres of land under cultivation. A homestead proved up at the end of five years. The only expense was for making out and recording the "patent." But Manly does not know how much that was. It was a patent from the government, not a deed. If a man wanted to prove up before five years ended, he could do so by paying $1.25 an acre."

**Eliza Jane**

When I came to Virginia last August the pulse was only 52. And the whole system, nervous and physical, was at a low ebb. My physician assures me 'twould be folly to think again of trying to live alone in my present state of health, even surrounded by the comforts and even luxuries of life, without exposing myself to the unavoidable hardships of that climate. If Our Honorable Land Commissioner could be persuaded to spend six weeks in winter alone in one of those Dakota houses with no living being to speak to except his dog and perhaps his horses. No earthly employment except to cook his food, keep fires and feed his team knowing that not many miles away there was plenty of work at good pay and comfortable homes.

# JJJ. Miss Wilder of DeSmet

Though E.J.'s homestead nearly adjoined the town of DeSmet and she could sit in her doorway and observe the activities of the new cluster of houses, buildings and businesses of the townsite, she said very little of the new community in her homesteading account. But though it is not mentioned by E.J. herself, she was an important asset to the fledgling DeSmet.

As in any struggling settlement in the west, the abilities and contributions of competent citizens were eagerly sought, and Miss Wilder was soon identified as a woman of talent and capability, a resource to fill a variety of roles. As she mentioned, she taught school with reluctance, but nevertheless she retained a concern for her profession and her name appears on the roles for Teacher's Institute training sessions for several years after she taught the DeSmet school. And though she preferred to devote her energies to the improvement of her farm rather than spend time in the settlement, E.J. invited into the social life of DeSmet -- the church, the Sunday School, the temperance society and other beginnings of cultural activity.

With the flurry of legal documents and recording of land transactions sometimes overwhelming the newly formed Kingsbury County offices, E.J. found periodic employment as a copyist and examples of her delicate penmanship can yet be found in musty old legal records of the 1880s. And for her brothers E.J. could act as secretary . . .

With both Royal and Almanzo far more canny with a team of horses or a walking plow than with a pen, the boys asked their sister to write a letter to their neighbor Dr. Cameron, (whose land adjoined the Wilder claims) asking for permission to cut some of the doctor's wild hay. This E.J. did, mailing the letter to the doctor in Sioux Falls, but neglecting to enclose a postage stamp for his return reply. Back came the doctor's answer, saying nothing about the hay, but demanding, "Where in hell is your postage stamp!"

Eliza Jane, spurred into a sparring match, promptly mailed back the answer to the location of the stamp by saying, "It's to the left of the furnace door; you will see it as **you go in.**" The doctor's next reply

---

*In addition to her homestead, E.J. invested in other DeSmet property. Kingsbury County Courthouse records show that "on June 22, 1886, Miss E.J. Wilder, an unmarried woman, sold through A.A. Wilder, attorney of Fillmore County, Minnesota, Lot 12, in Block 10 to Mrs. Caroline L. Ingalls for $100." This is the lot on which Charles Ingalls built his family's permanent home. It is located on Third Street in DeSmet.*

24

**DeSmet in 1883**

mentioned nothing about postage stamps; it informed the Wilder brothers that they could cut whatever hay they wished from his homestead land!

Though Eliza Jane had led the Sunday School at Valley Springs, no evidence exists that she taught classes at DeSmet's Congregational Church, though she herself attended classes and became a favored friend of both the Reverend Edward Brown and his wife Laura. (Both husband and wife made long, poetical presentations to E.J. in her autograph album on November 25, 1882). She also became active in the local Women's Christian Temperance Union and a **DeSmet Leader** news item in July, 1885, reported that "E.J. Wilder is superintendent of the department of unfermented wine at the Lord's table."

Another mention of E.J. in the columns of the **DeSmet Leader** illustrates the link between town and country which she forged while homesteading. "The Leader's thanks are due to Miss Eliza Wilder for supplying the editor's family with some delicious pie-plant," reads a report made during the spring of 1884. As a farmer's daughter, E.J. knew that the luxury of a garden in the country naturally must be shared with less fortunate friends who lived along a town streets!

25

# IV. Government Girl

"Back-trailer" was the term Hamlin Garland gave to homesteaders who tasted western life but returned to a more "civilized" existence in the east. Garland himself tried Dakota homesteading, but rejected it for the educational and cultural opportunities he craved in the eastern cities. Eliza Jane, too, headed east when she closed the door on her claim shanty and admitted that homesteading alone was too formidable challenge.

While E.J. rested and recuperated at her parents' farm in Spring Valley, she concocted a plan. She must resume the single woman's dilemma of supporting herself; slipping into the fabric of life at home as the spinster sister did not appeal to her. Occupations as rigorous as farming had to be forgotten; E.J. needed to find steady employment which could utilize her considerable skills and general adaptability. She decided to travel to Washington, D.C. and join the working force known as "government girls."

No documentation remains which pinpoints the source of E.J.'s employment decision, but her autograph album chronicles the trip east in 1887 and her autumn visit in Richmond and Bon Air, Virginia. Friends and acquantances who signed their names to the book wished E.J. "a pleasant trip to Washington" and hopes for her future employment.* The eastern friends had heard fascinating tales of Dakota homesteading, for several mentions were made of "Miss Wilder in her western home." Although she was preparing to settle in the city of Washington, the prairies still haunted E.J.

Early in 1888, E.J. successfully passed the civil service examination, and her score was complimented by Alfred Edgerton of the testing commission. "Let all your purposes," he wrote, "be as high as your grade in your Civil Service Examination and it will ever be well with you." With that ponderous blessing, E.J. took her desk in the Appointments Division of the Department of the Interior, then naturally a predominately male-operated office. There E.J. typed, filed records, did errands and filled the early-day duties of the secretary.

A letter to her father, typed on "office time," is a vignette showing E.J.'s general contentment with her life in Washington . . .

---

*Intriguing is the flourishing signature of Fitzhugh Lee in E.J.'s album. Lee, the elder brother of General Robert E. Lee, was governor of Virginia when he signed the album on November 28, 1887. Unfortunately, no stories survive which detail E.J.'s meeting with the Governor.

*My Dear Father:*

*Your good letter came in due season and was very welcome. I have it not by me so may not answer all the questions. I am sorry you and mother do not decide to spend the summer with me but perhaps you will be happier where you are. I like Washington very much. It does not seem like a city to me, the streets are so wide and there are so few in them in summer. In winter there is of course a crowd but still not crowded. I trust you are all well and happy as can be expected. I have not heard from any of you since the news of Aunt Delia's death. No doubt you are all very busy.*

*I had a paper from R.L. Austin yesterday. I would not wonder that Booming Ocosta proved to be a good investment. I will send the paper soon. I desire to show it to some people here first. I send an express order for $100 to apply on the debts. I should have sent it sooner but some way expenses keep pace with income always. I hoped to get an increase of salary but cannot this spring. You speak of living on borrowed time. I surely hope there will be many years loaned you. Why, you are a comparatively young man yet. I guess not quite that but the man where I board is 82 now and my best friend here is a lady 84 and there seems many years before then both.* ***

*Is there any way of finding out if the freight on a box of oranges would cost more than they are worth? I would like to send you a box. I suppose I ought to go and see if there is any work for me to do for Uncle Sam so goodbye. Write me as often as you feel like it. The letters are always welcome.*

*Goodbye. With love to all.*

*Your loving daughter, E.J. Wilder*

In the capital city it is not surprising that E.J. found sympathetic ears for her opinions on the equal rights movement, and avenues of expanding her energies as a suffragist. Among her friends were two leaders of the feminist movement, Dr. Mary Walker and Mrs. Amelia Bloomer, both of whom understood E.J.'s daring in the adventure of homesteading singlehandedly in the west. Dr. Walker and Mrs. Bloomer empathized with females who cut ties with expected roles for women; Dr. Walker was the first commissioned woman surgeon during the Civil War and Mrs. Bloomer pioneered the votes-for-women movement. Both of E.J.'s friends advocated dress reform; the

***E.J.'s autograph book names her meeting "best friend here" as Sarah A. Tyler, and sure enough, she was 84. Her 1806 birthdate was inscribed next to her name.*

27

doctor was arrested frequently by authorities who disapproved of her black frock men's suit attire and Mrs. Bloomer's name of course became immortalized in the ankle-length pants and tunic she wore and publicized as a welcome respite from swaying hoop-skirts, layers of crinoline and bulky dresses.

On her regular vacations from her government office E.J. resumed her pleasure of traveling to visit friends and family. Her vacation in 1889 included a stay with her lawyer-cousin and his family in New York City, the Edward Wilders, and she traveled to Spring Valley to see her parents. In the summer of 1890 E.J. arrived home to find Almanzo, Laura and their three-year old Rose making an extended stay on the farm. The summer canning season was in full swing and the big kitchen was full of women and heat and activity and the sound of E.J.'s voice discussing farm reform and women's rights. Laura remembered that good Mother Wilder "still the undisputed head of her household" was not a "feminist." Laura recalled: "I never heard the words 'economic independence' on her lips and when her daughter, who went to the city and worked in an office came back to talk of these things, she listened with an indulgent smile. She was too busy to bother her head with such notions, she said."

Reform other than the feminist questions buzzed in E.J.'s head that summer of 1890. Interrupting her Spring Valley stay, she went to DeSmet on "a mission to her brother farmers in Dakota." She had closely studied the farm platform in Washington and knew Dakota farmers were suffering not only from drought but from high interest, a protective tariff, falling prices and inadequate storage for previous bumper crops.* E.J.'s aim was to share her insights from Washington's viewpoint and offer her opinions on the cause of general hard times on the plains. Unable to reach as many DeSmet farmers as she wished while in town, she gathered her thoughts and penned an opinionated, tart editorial which she sent to C.P. Sherwood for publication in his **DeSmet Leader.** The letter appeared,** a testimony then and now to E.J.'s intelligent examination of public affairs and her staunch loyalty to Dakota and her "brother farmers" . . .

*All of these problems led to the Populist movement shortly after.

**Ironically, E.J.'s letter came to light 83 years after it was published during the restoration of the Ingalls home in DeSmet. While repairing the plaster in Mary Ingalls' bedroom, layers of old newspapers were discovered pasted over studding inside the walls. On closer examination, the letter signed "E.J. Wilder" was found. The section of wall, with E.J.'s editorial in plain sight, was covered with glass and is seen by the annual tourist crowds who visit DeSmet and the Ingalls house.

From the National Capital.
WASHINGTON, D.C.,
July 18, '90.

ED. LEADER: When I went to DeSmet it was my intention to find an opportunity to speak to the farmers upon some of the most important questions of the hour, but I was so much interested in seeing and hearing you all that I forgot that part of my mission until the morning of my departure, therefore I beg space in your columns for a few thoughts.

Every one seems to attribute the hard times to this lack of money and the failure of crops. But I fear that all do not know that the stringency of the money market is not due to high tariff, but to the fact that for years the United States has loaned money to the banks at one percent, accepting U.S. Bonds as security. Now the bonds are being paid off and premium is so high that new banks are not being opening and the money therefore accumulates in the treasury as there is not other authorized method of distribution except through pension and other appropriations. The result is that there is not enough money in circulation to do the business of the country and therefore prices are low.

Senator Stanford's measure to loan the money upon real estate security is opposed. I fear by many farmers, upon the ground that it is unconstitutional or the security is not good. If we have the right under the constitution to loan money to corporations we have also the right to loan it to the people individually.

If the whole country was one vast frog pond or if every farmer would unite in refusing to sow or reap for two years U.S. bonds would be worthless. Is not the land then the basis of value, and better security than the bonds?

The Sub-Treasury Bill I believe proposes to build store-houses and loan the farmer 80 percent of the value of his crop providing he stores it in these ware-houses, and agrees to forfit the crop unless redeemed within one year. A magnificent scheme for the speculators as they can easily visit these ware-houses and know exactly how much grain there is in the country, and as the time of redemption draws near force a still more stringent money market, thus keeping the price so low the farmer can not sell making it impossible to borrow the money needed for redemption and thus buy up these receipts for a small sum, then up go the prices and the poor farmer sees that he has been fleeced by the very parties whom he thought to trust. There are so many other potent objections to this storehouse plan that I feel sure the intelligent farmers of Dakota will refuse this sugar coated pill.

About the failure of crop you must all agree that the lack of rain is almost the only source of fear. Could you control the supply of water there is no more fertile land under heavens blue dome than our own beloved Dakota.

Senator Moody spoke for nearly two hours yesterday before the senate upon the question of artesian wells. He handled the subject in a manner which compelled careful, interested and earnest attention from his colleagues. And when we called upon him tonight we found him suffering from hoarseness the result of a cold contracted during the exhaustion attendant upon such an effort in the intense heat of such a day as was yesterday. But the senator refuses to rest and hopes to get an appropriation to continue the investigation and put down three or four experiment wells.

I am not a politician or much of a financer, but I do love my brother farmers of Dakota and would not a few artesian wells do more for the brave pioneers of Kingsbury than all the stuff and nonsense about farm reform. U.S. ware-houses and the thousand and one "Will o' the wisps" that are held out as decoys by wily politicians to blind the farmer to his own interest for their personal aggrandizement?

E.J. Wilder

Miss E.J. Wilder returned to Minnesota Monday, after a few days spent visiting old friends here. Miss Wilder is employed in the pension office at Washington, at a good paying salary. As her appointment is under the civil service rules, she counts upon a permanent position.

29

Eliza Jane was now in her early forties and her position in the pension office might have continued until she, too could draw a government pension. But that did not happen. Around 1892 E.J. terminated her job as "government girl" and returned to Spring Valley. Just as she was a person of many capabilities, she was also a woman who thrived on abrupt changes . . . and leaving Washington for the Minnesota farm resulted in E.J.'s most conventional role: wife and mother.

Co-workers sign E.J.'s autograph book

# V. Latter-Day Wife and Mother

Eliza Jane was not long on the Spring Valley farm when she began to be courted by--as Rose Wilder Lane described him--"an older, rich, retired gentleman-planter of Crowley, Louisiana." E.J.'s suitor was indeed older; Thomas Jefferson Thayer was past sixty, when on a visit to Spring Valley he offered his attentions to James Wilder's daughter. Indeed, the Wilders knew Tom Thayer well. He had lived near Malone at Thayer's Corners, and after moving west became known as Spring Valley as a prosperous pioneer merchant and grain elevator owner.

Mr. Thayer was a family man, but a man without a wife when E.J.'s interest was first kindled in the courtly-looking white-haired gentleman. His first wife had died in Spring Valley the year E.J. went west to Dakota and a second wife died in Crowley, leaving her husband a six year old daughter named Etta. With some of his first family of five grown children Mr. Thayer had entered into the rice-raising business in Louisiana and had increased his sizeable estate by a boom in the "rice capital" of Crowley.

And so, after ventures far and wide and a variety of varied experiences, E.J. decided to assume the role of wife, homemaker and mother to the little Etta. She would be saying farewell to Spring Valley once more, for the Thayers were established in Crowley, but the wedding was planned at the Wilder farm for September 6, 1893. The farm had been the scene of a gala golden wedding lawn party for E.J.'s parents exactly a month earlier, and the outdoor atmosphere was re-created for the Wednesday wedding. Behind the house was a grove of oaks; among them a picturesque bower was erected to frame the bride and groom during the ceremonies.

In 1976, this writer was privileged to interview the last remaining guest at E.J. and Tom Thayer's wedding. She was the 88-year-old Mabel Lamson, who remembered the occasion well. Mabel was a daughter of E.J.'s cousin Chet Lamson, and as a rosy five-year-old she was among the little girls who acted as flower girls and attendants to their much-older cousin. The wedding party was apparently very formal in the standards of rural Minnesota of the 1890s, and the banquet was one of Mother Wilder's famous spreads of country kitchen cookery.

The Thayers went immediately to Crowley to live and almost as soon, E.J.--Mrs. Thayer--was with child. She was 44, her husband 62, when their only child was born on June 15, 1894. He was a son and he was given proud old family names: Walcott for his paternal grandfather and his mother's maiden name as his second name. The boy was Walcott Wilder Thayer, but E.J. was pleased to have him called Wilder.

**Thomas Thayer, E.J.'s husband, whom Rose Wilder Lane described as "an older, rich, retired gentlemen."**

**Wilder, E.J.'s only child in 1905**

E.J. found life in the south to her liking, just as she had enthused over Dakota and Washington earlier. Despite her new role as a mother and wife, she wanted her Minnesota family around her and she wrote rhapsodizing about Louisiana. She urged her parents, her sister Laura (then a widow) and her brothers to pull up stakes and join her in Crowley. She knew that Almanzo and Royal were both in shaky health; she saw that Perley was looking for a locale to tie his fortunes; she felt that Laura and her parents should retire to the south. E.J. had been a book-saleslady and later she would again use her selling tactics, but now she eagerly worked to "sell" Louisiana.

Royal and Almanzo settled down in Spring Valley and Mansfield, Missouri respectively, but young Perley was lured by E.J.'s stories of fortune to be made in rice plantations. In January of 1895, he left Spring Valley, planning to settle in the south after looking over Texas, Cuba and Crowley. He decided on Louisiana and started farming rice on the Mermentau River. E.J. was delighted to have him near and having two of their children in the Crowley area helped to bait Father and Mother Wilder, then in their seventies and eighties.

Finally the elder Wilders decided to sell out in Spring Valley and retire in Crowley. Their daughter Laura planned to accompany them. E.J. had encouraged Laura's children to settle in Crowley and already the oldest girl Angie had married Fred Merritt in E.J.'s parlor. Selling their substantial Minnesota holdings took time, and it was 1898 before James and Angeline, with Laura, were ready to move. En route, they spent the summer with Almanzo, Laura and Rose who

32

were living in a rented house in the village of Mansfield. It was fall when E.J. welcomed them all to her home in Crowley.

There were a few months of happy reunion for the Wilders of Louisiana, which included now two of James and Angeline's daughters, their son Perley and several grandchildren, including E.J.'s four year old Wilder. But the pleasant times were few, because a string of tragedies soon occured. The first was financial; E.J. and Perley, no doubt with Tom Thayer's good advice, persuaded Father Wilder to invest a large portion of his considerable estate in a disastrous rice farming venture. E.J., sure of a quick profit, was horrified when the crop was a failure, and as one relative described it, "they had to give the crop away." Before she could rebound, E.J. was hit with the deaths of those closest to her.

On February 1, 1899 her father died while visiting at Perley's and no sooner than the family had returned from Old Crowley cemetery where Mr. Wilder was buried, Tom Thayer fell ill. A week later, at 67, he was dead. E.J., at 49 was left with a four-year old to raise alone. She soon learned how very much alone she would be.

Grief-stricken at the loss of father and husband, ugly threats began arriving from Tom Thayer's grown children. They claimed their father's entire estate, and legally they were entitled to all their father's assets through the Louisiana laws which still clung to the Napoleonic community-property law. As Rose Lane told it, Mr. Thayer "left E.J. a small son and nothing else . . . a widow was entitled to half of property accumulated **during the marriage,** and Mr. Thayer, retired, and had accumulated none. His children . . . took everthing, even E.J.'s wedding ring. The court, however gave her son a child's tenth and gave her his guardianship and a tiny allowance as his nurse."

E.J. tried to fight the unfairness of the situation, even engaging the assistance of her cousin in New York City, Lawyer Wilder. Cousin William did collect some funds for E.J., remarking that "I only wish that I could make out a large bill and collect every cent of it." He also commisserated with E.J., saying that "It is too bad you are having so hard a time. I can't understand why the Laws of Louisiana so discriminate against the widow."

In the midst of her legal difficulties, E.J.'s last remaining sister (Alice had died in 1892) died in September 1899 at Perley's home. It seemed that E.J.'s dreams of gathering the family in the south were turning to ashes; within the year both her father and sister had died, and E.J. was a widow with a five year old to rear.

Within their reduced circumstances, E.J. continued to live on in Crowley with Wilder. Her mother spent time with E.J. and also visited with Perley and her grandchildren. And during the summer of 1903, E.J. took Wilder for an extended stay with Almanzo, Laura and Rose in Mansfield. During the visit E.J. was quite taken with her niece Rose, whom she considered a **"very bright girl."** E.J. was correct; Rose Wilder was certainly what would today be termed "academically gifted" and the Mansfield village schools were no challenge to her natural inquisitiveness. Rose had long wished to study Latin, but her parents could not afford to send her to a private academy, so E.J. invited her back to Crowley. She could attend the Crowley high school and become acquainted with her Louisiana relatives as well.

As Rose tells it, the Crowley year with E.J. was a productive one . . .

*When I was 16 I went--was sent--to Crowley, to stay with my aunt and go to high school. There was no high school in Mansfield, and in Crowley it was only two grades -- 7th and 8th -- beyond McGuffey's Sixth Eclectic Reader. This was its first year. There were seven students in it. Having no classroom space for it, the Principal allowed us to study and recite in his office.*

*I had rarely, if ever, I believe never, finished a school year after we left Dakota when I was seven. In DeSmet I had finished Second Reader. In Mansfield I couldn't stand the stupid teachers, and there was no compulsion then; I just quit school. So to enter High School I had to pass examinations, in history English, American in Ancient history, in Literature, in Civics (political institutions), in geography, in mathematics, and in Latin. This I did brilliantly--having read a lot, including textbooks (there were not many other books in Mansfield) and spent a summer doing algebra problems in the hayloft, lying on my stomach on the hay and eating apples. Also, luckily, I had read English historical novels enough to pass the exam in English history.*

**E.J.'s Crowley home**

*But I had had no Latin, and to graduate I must do four years of that
--from Grammar to Caesar to Cicero, inclusive. And I lacked plane
geometry. (I never did know arithmetic, don't today; it was assumed
that I did because I made 100 in algebra). I insisted so forcefully that I
would do four years of Latin and make up the year of plane geometry
that the Principal agreed to enroll me in High School. Fortunately
the classes were so timed that I could sit in the classes of Grammar,
Advanced Grammar, and Caesar, and return to the Principal's Office
to study Cicero; also I could make the plane geometry class.*

*It was a wonderful year. We seven studied together in the comfor-
table office. The English teacher came in at the appointed hour to
teach us Shakespere's plays; the Principal came to hear our work in
Cicero and in solid geometry; the rest of the time was ours by
ourselves. I had no trouble with the studies and was tops from the
first in all Latin classes. Because I was **using** grammar before learning
it, which I'm convinced is the only way to learn it. I started right in
blithely, writing the Latin words down the left side of the paper*

| | |
|---|---|
| *arma* | *arms* |
| *virumque* | *and man* |
| *cano* | *I sing* |
| *qui* | *who* |
| *prima* | *first* |
| *ab* | *etc.* |
| *oris* | |

*Then, looking them up in the dictionary and the grammar and who
COULDN'T then translate it to: I sing of arms and a man who first
from the shores of Italy . . . ?? And after about ten pages of this, I was
sailing through Latin translations with rarely a pause for dictionary
or grammar. I graduated from High School at the TOP of FOUR
classes in Latin, and wrote a poem in Latin for the "graduating exercises."*

*Well, before Thanksgiving I had two or three of what used to be
called suitors, and by Thanksgiving my heart belonged to -- is it funny
or sad that I can't remember his name? He was Prince Charming, the
only one I have ever known. He was from Chicago, he was visiting
his sister, he was an Older Man, a graduate of the University of
Chicago, he must have been all of 24 years old; his manners were
polished until they glittered, he drove a phaeton and pair, he owned
evening dress (nowhere to wear it in Crowley, but he showed me a
picture of himself in it, in Chicago. In fact, he gave me the picture; I
treasured it for years and years -- for at least two years. He drove me
to school every morning, in the phaeton. Every evening after school
he was waiting for me, in the phaeton. It had red wheels, rubber tired.*

*I hurriedly left my books at my aunt's (she was out of her mind about me, fearing the worst of my virtue) and we were off deliriously for the evening. We ate in* **restaurants.** *We drove for hours and miles along those dusty white roads in the moonlight, betwen the cypress tress dripping Spanish moss, by the gleaming dark bayous where the aligators slept in piles, past the rice fields and through the sleeping tiny towns . . . My virtue was not at all endangered. I MUST be in by 10. And almost always I was at my aunt's by midnight.*

*Now to work. There was a long screened porch, buried in vines, along the side of the house by my room--porch called in Louisiana a gallery. There I had a table under the light, with my books on it. I did the exercises in Latin grammar, I did the lesson in Caesar and the lesson in Cicero, and I could not keep my eyes open. I must be brightly up before sunrise, to curl my hair, etc., etc., and be ready before HE came to drive me to school. And I don't remember how I discovered a way to do next day's geometry problems. But I did, and it worked for the rest of the school year. This way:*

*LOOK at the problem: to bisect the cone . . . Set the alarm clock two minutes ahead. Sleep. (I had only to stop trying to keep my eyes open, let my head down to the table.) Bong! the alarm! You're awake, to bisect the cone . . . Get the solution down on paper. LOOK at the next problem and repeat. In 12 minutes--oh, say 15.--the six problems were solved. I was sleeping on my bed until the alarm woke me to tomorrow and the beau in the phaeton. On the way to school I read the solutions -- the geometry class was the first of the day. And I got grades in math, as well as in Latin. I worked all the problems while I slept, and always got correct solutions.*

*The oddest thing, it seems to me now, is that I took all this for granted, never thought about it. I just did it. We had a discussion, the seven of us in the Principal's office, about getting a Latin "pony." Would it be ethical to use one? Though perhaps using a translation to help us to learn the language, IF we honestly used it to* **learn** *and honestly* **knew** *the lessons, might not be wrong, we decided, No. There seemed to be something rather sneaky about it, unless we first asked the Principal? We discussed that, but none of us wanted to do that, for some reason. So the boy who had been offered the "pony" refused it. The question of whether I earned my grades in math never occurred to me.*

E.J. and Rose enjoyed each other famously and both appreciated the other's independent natures. E.J. was actively supporting Eugene V. Debs and his Social Democratic Party (soon to become the "Wobblies", the Industrial Workers of the World) and among Rose's memories of the Crowley year were political meetings and handing

A Crowley
photographer
recorded Rose's
graduation pose,
during the
spring of the
year she spent
with E.J.

out Debs literature with her Aunt E.J. Rose also adopted her aunt's strong feminist views and certainly when Rose returned home after her graduation, she left Crowley with a large dose of E.J.'s influence.

Rose went home to Mansfield but not permanently. Soon she had learned telegraphy and was hired by Western Union in Kansas City where she participated in the first nation-wide walk-out. Like E.J. Rose espoused dress reform -- cutting her hair short, wearing a man's shirt with a "skirt that actually cleared the dirty city sidewalk." E.J. lived to see Rose plunge into the business world, become a nationally famous writer and world traveler and she was proud of her niece. Rose, too, was proud of her father's sister and more than once the character of Aunt E.J. slipped into personages in Rose's fiction.

# VI. Louisiana Lady

After Rose graduated and returned to Mansfield, E.J. completed her plans to marry a man she met through her political work for Debs. That unflagging campaigning had netted E.J. a gold watch as a testimonial, but more important, it yielded a new husband. He was Maxwell Gordon, whose poetical, dreamy character appealed to E.J. They were married in Crowley on July 1, 1904.

Along with her new husband, E.J. entered into a business venture -- she always had leaned toward commerce, no matter how small a scale -- and bolstered with a $500 legacy from her father's estate* the Gordons went to Texas. In Brownsville they opened a combination fruit-stand-souvenir stand. Wilder, at thirteen, was photographed with two Missouri soldiers in front of the well-stocked store front.

In January of 1908, E.J. was visiting in Crowley with her niece Angie Merritt and her "five fine children." In a letter she wrote to a cousin in Malone, E.J. mentioned that "I had to break up housekeeping and go to Marlin, Texas, this fall. I was getting almost paralyzed. Am better but not much. I shall go to housekeeping soon." From these anecdotes, it sounds doubtful that the business in Brownsville was very long-lived or profitable. Nor was E.J.'s second marriage.

**The fruit-stand and souvenir shop which E.J. and Max Gordon operated in Brownsville, Texas in 1907. Son Wilder is posed with two Missouri soldiers.**

*Though Mother Wilder did not die until 1905, E.J., as administrator of James Wilder's estate, had distributed $500 inheritances to each of her brothers at the end of 1903.*

**E.J. at Christmas-
time, 1910**

Max Gordon, as the family remembers him, was an improvident man with illusions of poetic and literary ability which seemed always on the verge of realization. When E.J. was settled again in Louisiana, Max Gordon's disturbing financial situation and unsettled traits grew more evident. As he remarked, "I am of no value as a commercial asset and I felt it would only be a matter of time when I would be the cause of you losing your home." There was some hint of a scandal which Max referred to as a "cowardly attack on my character" and finally when "my honor was a stake and your happiness was in the balance," he disappeared.

By the time Max Gordon left, Wilder had finished his schooling and was seeking a career. Both he and his mother thought of Rose. Wilder had always idolized his older cousin, who by 1914 was married to Gillette Lane and selling real estate in California. Wilder, too, thought of moving to California, and he asked for Rose's advice. Rose was anxious to see her aunt and cousin, but she cautioned that "I don't want you to be building an erroneous idea of what I will be able to do. Neither do I want you to think anything except that I will do my darndest." Rose had herself just emerged from six months without a single real estate sale.

The elaborate motor-trip to visit Rose did not materialize for Wilder and E.J., but news did come from Max Gordon in California. "Deep down in the center of my intelligence I revere you and through the eternities I shall idealize your friendship," he wrote to E.J. from Colma, California. He had published a poem on Peace, he reported, and intended "to get out a book of Poems very soon, also a Book." Since he feared that "I shall never be back to the old South again" he asked E.J. for his "legal liberty," promising "never to marry again." Max asked for the divorce "for your sake as well as mine," and after his long desertion, E.J. could hardly object to the request. Later, the family heard that Max had taken his poetical skills to Australia.

With Wilder now reared and soon to enter the service during World War I, E.J. made her headquarters with her faithful brother Perley and his family. Perley, his wife Elsie and their children had left their rice farm near Mermentau River and moved to Jeff Davis Parish where a railroad flagstop locale called Cloverdale and Lauderdale boasted a store-postoffice-railway depot. Perley was in charge of all three operations as well as the rice warehouses and his family made room for the aging Aunt E.J. As Perley's daughter Gladys recalls: "I suppose she was an near as we came to having a grandma because we never knew any of our grandparents . . ."

At the time she called Perley's house her home, E.J. was the "Fitch Soap Lady". She went door-to-door selling the strong soap, advertised as made from "pure coconut oil." Indeed it was potent; E.J.'s nephew James Wilder says that "two or three rubs gave a whole panful of soap". While all the relatives bought her product to help out their aunt, the children all hated using the soap. Along with her cleaning products, E.J. touted a gadget called "Men-d-ets", used to stop leaks in pots and pans. E.J., with her forceful sales pitch, often was able to demonstrate the patching device as well as sell the sudsy soap.

Gladys Wilder accompanied her aunt on one memorable selling excursion to the thriving saw-mill town of Einad. Retiring for the night in a local boarding house before the day of salesmanship, E.J. and Gladys were horrified to hear an onrush of bedbugs every time the lamp was darkened. They put in a sleepless night and with shades of her "nervous horror of bugs" experienced during Dakota days, E.J. cut the trip short and hustled home with Gladys. On their arrival Perley's wife promptly had them strip and thoroughly scrub down. Their clothes were boiled so that no nasty souvenirs of the boarding house mattresses would infest the Wilder house.

James Wilder also became involved in his aunt's selling trips when she had an appointment in Lafayette and needed to catch the Southern Pacific train into town. A rain storm had flooded the roads, making them all but invisible, but dauntless E.J. and James set out in a Model T. Muddy water swirled up to the running boards and the trip included the rescue of some stranded motorists, but E.J. was determined to meet her appointed business meeting.

E.J. was still living with Perley and his family when Wilder married. His bride was Frances Cockrell and the wedding occurred on March 18, 1918 at Lafayette. Wilder just escaped military duty overseas, when just before his sailing the Armistice ending World War I was signed. The young couple settled in Lafayette, and another new generation of Wilder descendants soon started.

# VII. Grandma Gordon

It is not surprising that E.J. followed Wilder and his wife to live in Lafayette. Family had always been her prop and support and she had given much in return. She had sacrificed to provide a home and education for Wilder. Keeping boarders, doing office work for an attorney and walking door-to-door to peddle her household products had all been tried through lean years of widowhood and later when Max Gordon proved to be "no commercial asset."

E.J. was able to establish her own home in Lafayette, which stood on the edge of a deep ravine. Wilder had gone to work for the Post Office and one by one, children began arriving. Walter Wilder was born in 1921; Francis Gervaise in 1922; Bettie in 1925 and Thomas in 1928. The older children remember their "Grandma Gordon" well.

Living alone in her little house, she was delighted when the grandchildren came to visit. Bettie recalls E.J.'s house as a wonderful stop midway between school and home in the afternoons. There were cookies and milk, but there was also afterschool learning. Grandma, she learned, had been a teacher long ago and she still liked keeping a school. From a thicket of berry bushes behind her house, E.J. made "invisible ink" from the crushed berries. This made learning and practicing her letters a delightful adventure for Bettie. Mysteriously E.J. would make the writing disappear, then re-appear when heated with a candle flame. As her grandsons grew older, they too learned to know a grandmother with stories to tell from her long and varied life on farms, offices, homestead claims, rice plantations, little towns and big towns in many places, over many years. The children realized that Grandma Gordon could be a bit strict and precise, stood for no silliness, but was full of love for them.

E.J. was eighty when she became ill in February, 1930. In the next months, she suffered two strokes, and was bedridden at Wilder's home recuperating. But the independent old pioneer did not recover. On June 1, 1930 she died. She was buried the next day in the Protestant Cemetery in Lafayette.

"Life was a constant series of hardships," mourned one old pioneer woman of her years on the prairie and certainly Eliza Jane Wilder could echo the words about her own life. But she would perhaps prefer to be remembered by her own challenge: "What amount of hardship can daunt the spirit of a native born American?" Spirit she had--as a feminist, a farmer, a family woman, a business woman--and that supreme self-confidence of E.J. Wilder is what makes her memorable yet today, as a literary character and as a grand example of a Victorian-era woman who said "I CAN!"

**Walter Thayer visits at Rocky Ridge Farm in Mansfield, Missouri with Uncle Manly (Almanzo Wilder) in 1938.**

# VIII. Postscript

E.J. did not live to see the 1933 publication of **Farmer Boy**, the story of her own family on the farm in Malone as told by her sister-in-law Laura Ingalls Wilder. And though she knew of her niece's prominent career as writer Rose Wilder Lane, she likewise did not live to see herself as a character in Rose's fiction. Doubtless, she would have enjoyed the recognition and had much to say in contributing to the stories told by her brother Almanzo's wife and daughter.

Wilder, her son, continued to live in Lafayette. With his wife and his cousin Bernice Granger (Royal's daughter), Wilder visited the Mansfield, Missouri farm where his cousin Rose and Uncle Manly lived. The first visit was in 1935; three years later Wilder returned with his children to see Laura and Almanzo.

**E.J. about the time of World War I - in a post which is reminiscent of her door-to-door saleslady job.**

Wilder lived out his life in Louisiana, described by Rose Wilder Lane to this writer as "apparently an important citizen of the town, and grandfather of numerous progeny." Indeed, by the time he retired from the postal service, he had a dozen grandchildren. He was well aware of his mother's status as a personage in children's literature through the "Little House" books and on a visit to his daughter Bettie's home in California he went to Pomona to see the Laura Ingalls Wilder Room of the library there.

Enjoying the good weather in Mexico City, Wilder Thayer spent much of his time there, but was back in Lafayette in the fall of 1965. Puttering around his house, he fell from a ladder. He died as the result of his accident. Today, the four Thayer children, their children and grandchildren comprise a large group of direct descendants of the indomitable Eliza Jane. They are fascinated with their link to the history and draw inspiration from a long legacy of pioneering spirit.

## About the editor . . .

William Anderson brings years of involvement with the Laura Ingalls Wilder legacy to the editing task of *A Wilder in the West*. His extensive research on the backgrounds of the Ingalls and Wilder families have resulted in a voluminous list of publications, lectures, workshops and visits to the Wilder locales. He was active in the early development of the Laura Ingalls Wilder Memorial Society in DeSmet, S.D., serving as tour director, researcher and historical interpreter. He founded and continues to edit the Society's newsletter, "Laura Ingalls Wilder Lore."

As a graduate of Albion College (B.A.) and South Dakota State University (M.A.), he combines a teaching career with continued research and writing. His works have appeared in *The Saturday Evening Post, American History Illustrated, The American West, Travel and Leisure, South Dakota History* and other publications. For historical writing on the Wilders, he was awarded the Robinson Award of the South Dakota State Historical Society and the Billington Award of the Western History Association in 1984.

His other biographies on "Little House" characters include: *The Story of the Ingalls, The Story of the Wilders, Laura Wilder of Mansfield, Laura's Rose: The Story of Rose Wilder Lane* and *The Ingalls Family Album.*